A Kalmus Classic Edition

Johannes
BRAHMS

EIN DEUTSCHES REQUIEM
A GERMAN REQUIEM

Opus 45

for Soprano and Baritone Soli, Chorus,
Orchestra and Organ (ad lib)
with German text and English text
in the preface

CHORAL SCORE

K 06110

Kalmus

JOHANNES BRAHMS

EIN DEUTSCHES REQUIEM

INHALT

A German Requiem

I

Blessed are they that mourn, for they shall have comfort.

They that sow in tears shall reap in joy.

Who goeth forth and weepeth, and beareth precious seed, shall doubtless return with rejoicing, and bring his sheaves with him.

II

Behold, all flesh is as the grass, and all the goodliness of man is as the flower of grass; for lo, the grass with'reth, and the flower thereof decayeth.

Now, therefore, be patient, O my brethren, unto the coming of Christ.

See how the husbandman waiteth for the precious fruit of the earth, and hath long patience for it, until he receive the early rain and the latter rain.

So be ye patient.

Albeit the Lord's word endureth for evermore.

The redeemed of the Lord shall return again, and come rejoicing unto Zion; gladness, joy everlasting, joy upon their heads shall be; joy and gladness, these shall be their portion, and tears and sighing shall flee from them.

III

Lord, make me to know the measure of my days on earth, to consider my frailty that I must perish.

Surely, all my days here are as an handbreadth to Thee, and my lifetime is as naught to Thee.

Verily, mankind walketh in a vain show, and their best state is vanity.

Man passeth away like a shadow, he is disquieted in vain, he heapeth up riches, and cannot tell who shall gather them.

Now, Lord, O, what do I wait for?

My hope is in Thee.

But the righteous souls are in the hand of God, nor pain, nor grief shall nigh them come.

IV

How lovely is Thy dwelling place, O Lord of Hosts!

For my soul, it longeth, yea fainteth for the courts of the Lord; my soul and body crieth out, yea, for the living God.

O blest are they that dwell within Thy house; they praise Thy name evermore!

V

Ye now are sorrowful, howbeit ye shall again behold me, and your heart shall be joyful, and your joy no man taketh from you.

Yea, I will comfort you, as one whom his own mother comforteth.

Look upon me; ye know that for a little time labor and sorrow were mine, but at the last I have found comfort.

VI

Here on earth have we no continuing place, howbeit, we seek one to come.

Lo, I unfold unto you a mystery.

We shall not all sleep when He cometh, but we shall all be changed in a moment, in a twinkling of an eye, at the sound of the trumpet.

For the trumpet shall sound, and the dead shall be raised incorruptible, and all we shall be changed.

Then, what of old was written, the same shall be brought to pass.

For death shall be swallowed in victory!

Death, O where is thy sting?

Grave, where is thy triumph?

Worthy art Thou to be praised, Lord of honor and might, for thou hast earth and heaven created, and for Thy good pleasure all things have their being, and were created.

VII

Blessed are the dead which die in the Lord from henceforth.

Sayeth the spirit, that they rest from their labors, and that their works follow after them.

Ein deutsches Requiem

1.

Johannes Brahms, Op. 45
(Veröffentlicht 1868)
Klavierauszug mit Text vom Komponisten

Ziemlich langsam und mit Ausdruck

2.

Langsam, marschmäßig

14

24

3.

Baß Solo

Ach, ___ wie gar nichts sind ___ al le Men schen, die doch so si cher le — — — — ben. Sie ge hen da her wie ein Sche — men, und machen ih — nen viel ver geb li che Un ru he; sie sammeln und wis sen

34

5.

6.

7.